HOW TO LIVE LIKE

A MEDIEVAL

KNIGHT

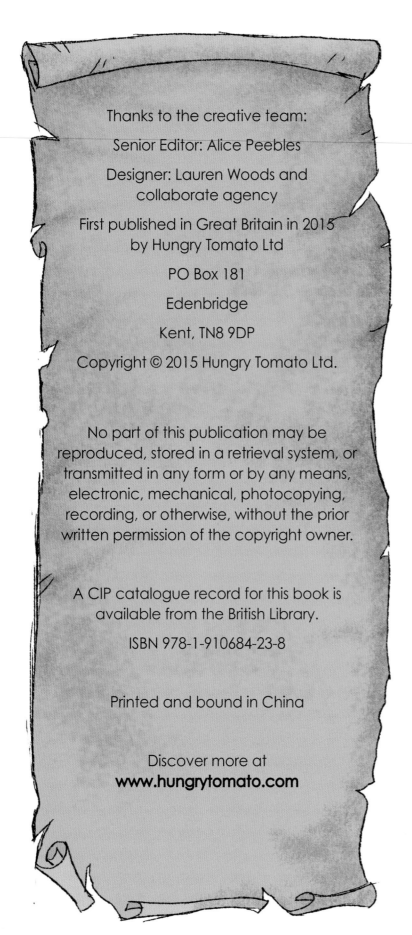

Thanks to the creative team:

Senior Editor: Alice Peebles

Designer: Lauren Woods and
collaborate agency

First published in Great Britain in 2015
by Hungry Tomato Ltd

PO Box 181

Edenbridge

Kent, TN8 9DP

A CIP catalogue record for this book is
available from the British Library.

ISBN 978-1-910684-23-8

Printed and bound in China

Discover more at
www.hungrytomato.com

HOW TO LIVE LIKE
A MEDIEVAL
KNIGHT

By Anita Ganeri

Illustrated by Mariano Epelbaum

HUNGRY
TOMATO™

Contents

Medieval Knight

It's the 14th century, and you've travelled back in time to the leafy town of Corfield in medieval England. I am Richard Marshall– squire in the service of my local lord, the Earl of Corfield. I've lived here since I was a page. Now my training is nearly finished and it'll soon be time to go off to war. Wish me luck.

What were the Middle Ages?

The Middle Ages is the name for a period of history in Europe, also called medieval times. It lasted from the fall of the Roman Empire around AD 500 to the beginning of the **Renaissance** the early 1300s.

What your life was like in the Middle Ages depended on your place in society. You were either free or unfree. Free people were barons or lords, knights, commoners (merchants, craftsmen and wage labourers),and freeholders (peasant farmers who owned their own farms).The unfree were the serfs (peasant farmers who did not own their land but worked for their lord).

Pope / Church

Monarch

Knights

Barons or Lords

Merchants

Craftsmen

Free- holders

Serfs

Wage labourers

Knights

Highly trained cavalrymen who fought for the king and his barons and lords in return for land

Barons and Lords

Ruled large areas of land for the king, and pledged their loyalty and lives to him

Monarch

Held supreme power in his own lands; often battled with other rulers abroad

Pope

Head of the Catholic Church in Rome; also had land and huge political power

Serfs

Lowest and largest class of people; worked a lord's land and were owned by him

Wage labourers

Free to travel, but did not own or work on their own land; they worked for other people for a day's wages

Merchants

Travelled far and wide to buy unusual or exotic goods that they traded at markets and fairs

Freeholders

Peasant farmers who owned their own land and farms, and paid tax to the king

Craftsmen

Blacksmiths, stone masons, carpenters and other skilled workers; together they formed groups called guilds

Knight in Training

Being a knight is something you inherit (my Dad was a knight, too). And it's all I ever wanted to be. When I was little, I used to spend hours every day riding on my hobby horse and spearing things with my toy lance – it was still sharp!

When I was seven, my Dad sent me away from home to live in the Earl of Corfield's household as a **page**. There wasn't time to feel homesick – I was too busy learning to ride a horse, fight with a sword and read and write. At 14 years old, I was ready to become a **squire** for another seven years.

WARNING!

You have to practise hitting the target with a wooden lance at first, until you're skilled enough to use a real one.

Training schedule

As a squire, my duties include waiting on my lord and his knights, serving them meals, looking after their horses, and keeping their armour and weapons clean. I've also been learning to handle different weapons, including swords and lances, on horseback and on foot. And there's still time for football and wrestling, to keep me fighting fit.

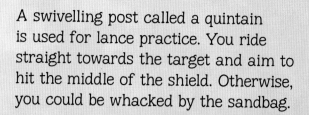

A swivelling post called a quintain is used for lance practice. You ride straight towards the target and aim to hit the middle of the shield. Otherwise, you could be whacked by the sandbag.

How to be chivalrous

Proper behaviour is as much part of being a knight as fighting skills. You have to follow a strict Code of **Chivalry**, which means you must...

1 Believe in God and the Church

2 Serve your Lord with courage and loyalty

3 Protect the weak and defenceless

4 Be honest and always tell the truth

5 Fight for the good of everyone

6 Guard the honour of your fellow knights

7 Never give up – see things through to the end

8 Never turn your back on your enemy

Life in the Castle

The earl's given me a day off from training, so let's go on a tour of Corfield Castle. As you know, I've lived here since I was seven years old, so it feels like home.

The castle started off as a **manor house** but was attacked a couple of times. The earl's father had permission from the king to fortify it and make it safer, so he added a thick new wall and battlements, and now it's easier to defend.

The entrance to the main gatehouse has wooden doors and an iron grill gate, called a portcullis. This can be lowered quickly, to keep attackers out.

Who lives here?

Apart from the knights, squires and pages, lots of people live in the castle. The most important are the lord, lady and their family, of course. Then there's the priest, steward (head servant), cook, butler, fletcher (arrow maker), carpenter, blacksmith, guards – and a crowd of others.

The castle is surrounded by a thick, stone wall with towers at regular intervals. Guards constantly patrol the walls. The battlements on top have squared openings that archers can fire through, then take cover. There are also arrows slits in the walls.

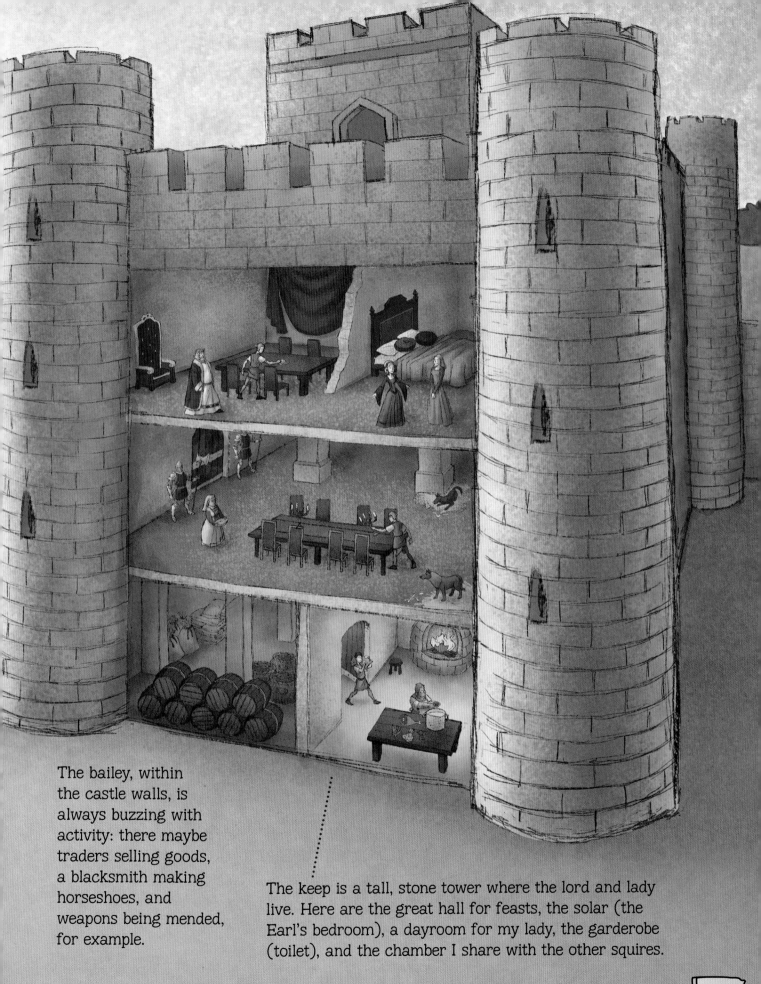

The bailey, within the castle walls, is always buzzing with activity: there maybe traders selling goods, a blacksmith making horseshoes, and weapons being mended, for example.

The keep is a tall, stone tower where the lord and lady live. Here are the great hall for feasts, the solar (the Earl's bedroom), a dayroom for my lady, the garderobe (toilet), and the chamber I share with the other squires.

'Arise, Sir Richard!'

There is no fixed age for becoming a knight. You'd usually be around 21 years old, but it depends on how your training goes and whether you (and your family) can afford to pay for your armour and warhorse.

At last! After all the training, the big day has arrived. My Lord has decided I am ready to become a knight. I had a long bath to wash away my sins. Then some of the other knights helped me get dressed in a red tunic, black stockings and a red cloak. Afterwards, I spent all night on my own praying in the chapel.

This morning, they fixed on my spurs and strapped on my special sword belt. The earl gave me my own sword and I knelt down in front of him and swore my **oath** of loyalty. He tapped me on each shoulder with his sword and said 'Arise, Sir Richard!'

How to get knighted on the eve of battle

If you find the whole ceremony too long and off-putting, try getting knighted before battle instead.

1 The king asks if anyone wants to become a knight.

2 You (and several others) step forward – it's a chance not to be missed.

3 You swear a short oath and get a quick tap on the shoulder.

4 That's it! Arise, Sir Knight!

In 1306, some 300 men were knighted in Westminster Abbey, England. Among them was the king's son, the future King Edward II. At a great feast afterwards, two (fake) swans were brought in on a platter and the knights swore their oaths on the birds.

The Black Prince

The eldest son of King Edward III, Prince Edward was a brilliant soldier and was knighted at the Battle of Crécy in France, in 1346, when he was just 16 years old. He was probably known as the Black Prince because of the colour of his armour.

William Wallace

Born in the 1270s, William became a hero in Scotland when he led a rebellion against Edward I and defeated the English at Stirling Bridge. He was made a Scottish knight in 1297, but Edward finally defeated his forces. The English pursued Wallace and took him prisoner. He was executed in 1305 and his head was stuck on a spike on London Bridge.

Arms and Armour

Now that I'm a fully fledged knight, I need to look the part. Battles (and tournaments) are dangerous places so it's vital to be well-protected. A good suit of armour is essential. I've been to the armourer to have one made (it cost me a fortune but it fits really well, which is also essential).

My steel-plate armour is strong and heavy, but it's well-made so is surprisingly easy to move in, once you've got it on. It does get horribly hot, though, especially as I'm wearing a padded cap, jacket and woolly leggings underneath. And the worst thing is, that it's difficult to see out when you're wearing your helmet.

Make sure you keep your armour in top condition – by oiling and polishing it regularly. This will stop it going rusty – after all rusty armour's no use to anyone.

Getting dressed

Putting on armour isn't easy, so give yourself plenty of time. Each piece must go on in the right order, starting with your sabatons (shoes) and finishing off with your great helm (helmet). You'll need your page or servant to help fasten all the buckles and tie all the laces.

Armour names

Each bit of your armour has a name that you'll need to know. After all, you don't want to mix up your cuisses (thigh guards) with your vambraces (arm guards), do you?

Weapons of war

Knights fight with a variety of weapons, including a lance and sword. Your sword is your most important weapon – it shouldn't be too heavy, and must always be kept sharp.

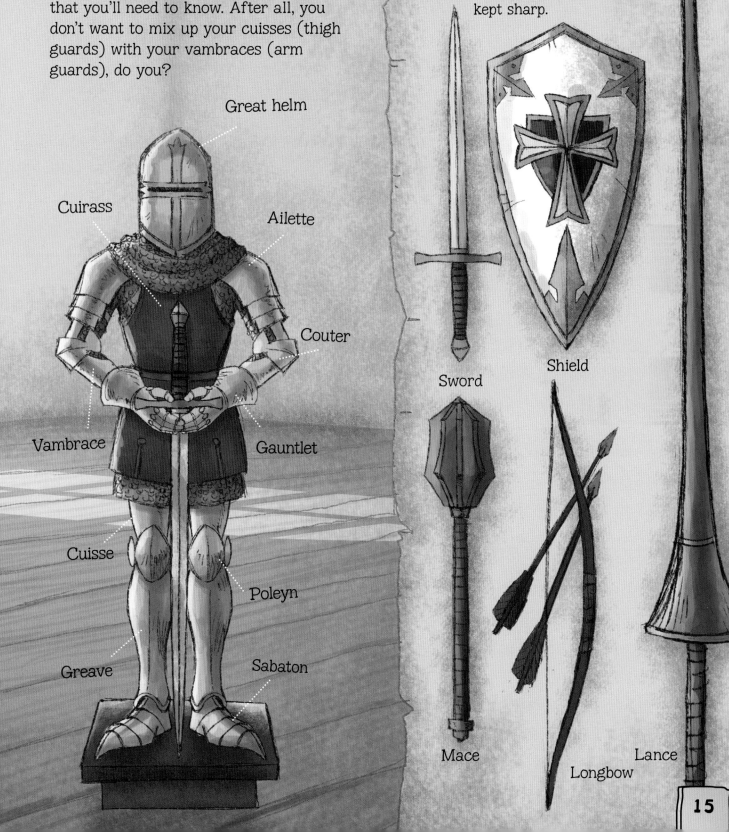

Great helm

Cuirass

Ailette

Couter

Vambrace

Gauntlet

Cuisse

Poleyn

Greave

Sabaton

Sword

Shield

Mace

Longbow

Lance

Tournament Time

So, I'm all dressed up and ready to go, but there aren't any battles to fight at the moment. Instead, the earl's holding a tournament – it's my first and I can't wait.

Tournaments are brilliant for showing off your fighting skills and keeping your wits sharp. I'm pretty handy with a lance so I've entered the jousting competition. I had to hang my shield up with the others – it's called 'entering the **lists**'. Anyway, the herald's just announced I'm on next. Right, helmet on, lance at the ready, and here goes. CHARGE!

How to design your own coat of arms

Knights in full armour are tricky to tell apart, so you need a coat of arms. This gets passed down through your family, so everyone knows who you are and where you come from. There's a wide range of colours and designs to choose from, all with their own meanings. Add a stirring motto, too, if you like.

WARNING!

Be careful! lances are dangerous weapons. Even though the ends are blunted, they can kill you or cause serious injury.

Helm

Mantle

Shield

MARSHALL

Surname

How to win at jousting

Each bout of jousting lasts for three rounds, and points are awarded as follows:

1 point – for hitting your opponent on his body

2 points – for hitting him so hard your lance snaps

3 points – for knocking him off his horse

If the points are even, the winner may be decided by a sword fight on foot.

If you knock your opponent clean off his horse, you win his horse and armour, or you might be given a title or some gold for bravery. But prizes aren't everything. Winning is always worth it for glory and honour alone.

Riding to Battle

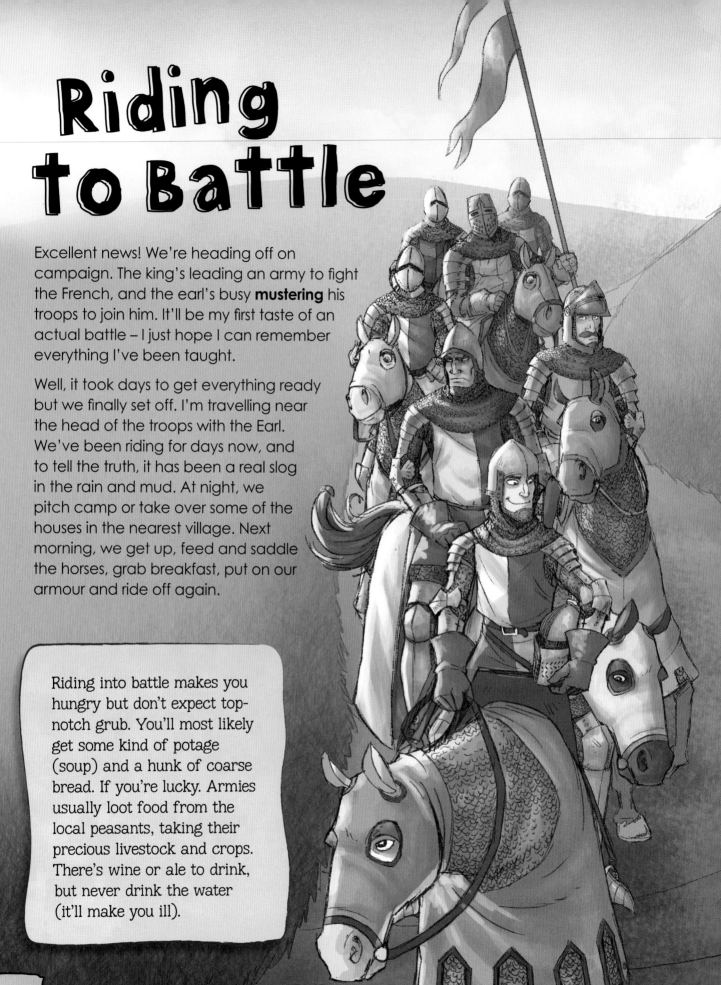

Excellent news! We're heading off on campaign. The king's leading an army to fight the French, and the earl's busy **mustering** his troops to join him. It'll be my first taste of an actual battle – I just hope I can remember everything I've been taught.

Well, it took days to get everything ready but we finally set off. I'm travelling near the head of the troops with the Earl. We've been riding for days now, and to tell the truth, it has been a real slog in the rain and mud. At night, we pitch camp or take over some of the houses in the nearest village. Next morning, we get up, feed and saddle the horses, grab breakfast, put on our armour and ride off again.

Riding into battle makes you hungry but don't expect top-notch grub. You'll most likely get some kind of potage (soup) and a hunk of coarse bread. If you're lucky. Armies usually loot food from the local peasants, taking their precious livestock and crops. There's wine or ale to drink, but never drink the water (it'll make you ill).

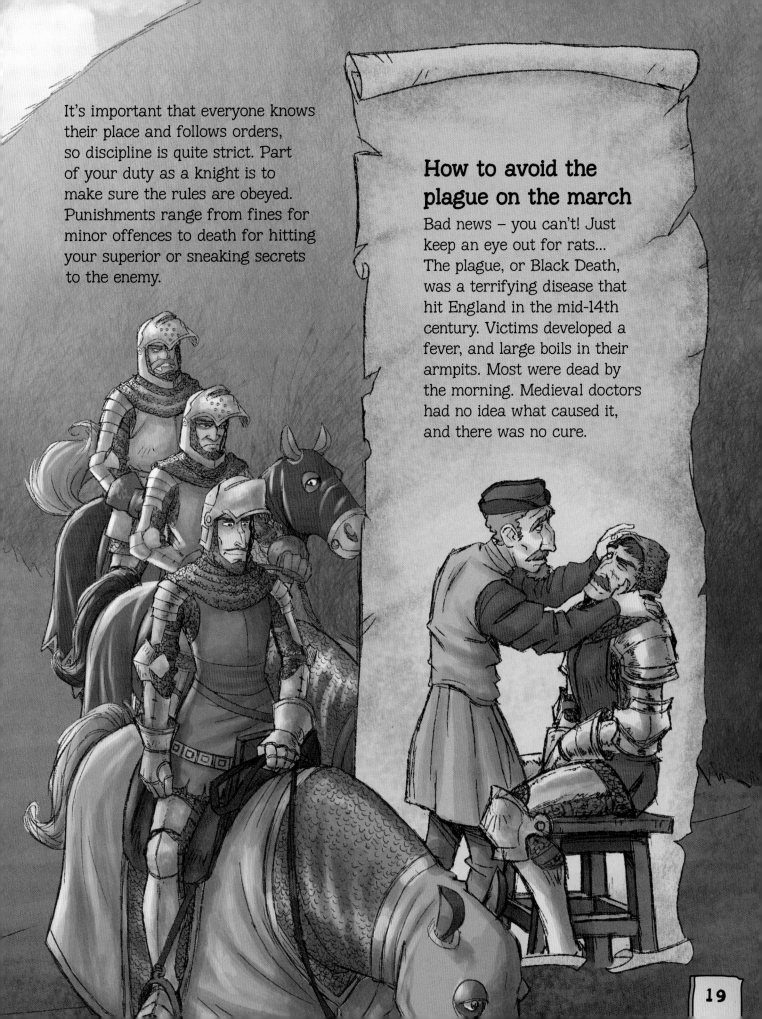

It's important that everyone knows their place and follows orders, so discipline is quite strict. Part of your duty as a knight is to make sure the rules are obeyed. Punishments range from fines for minor offences to death for hitting your superior or sneaking secrets to the enemy.

How to avoid the plague on the march

Bad news – you can't! Just keep an eye out for rats... The plague, or Black Death, was a terrifying disease that hit England in the mid-14th century. Victims developed a fever, and large boils in their armpits. Most were dead by the morning. Medieval doctors had no idea what caused it, and there was no cure.

Let Battle Begin!

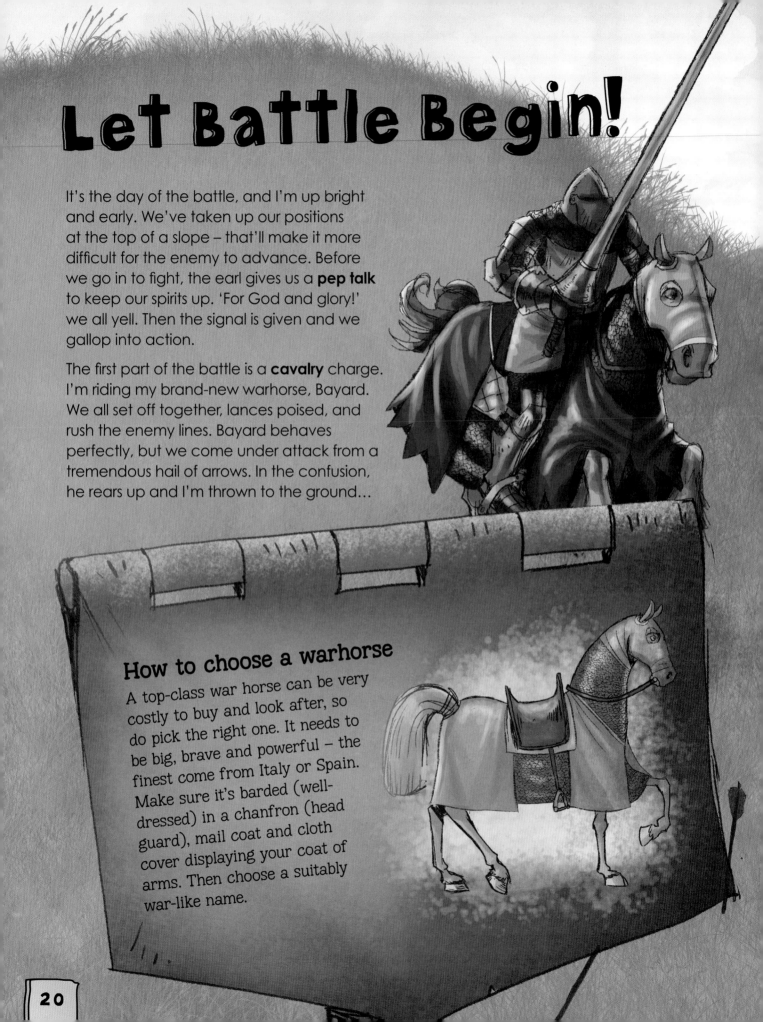

It's the day of the battle, and I'm up bright and early. We've taken up our positions at the top of a slope – that'll make it more difficult for the enemy to advance. Before we go in to fight, the earl gives us a **pep talk** to keep our spirits up. 'For God and glory!' we all yell. Then the signal is given and we gallop into action.

The first part of the battle is a **cavalry** charge. I'm riding my brand-new warhorse, Bayard. We all set off together, lances poised, and rush the enemy lines. Bayard behaves perfectly, but we come under attack from a tremendous hail of arrows. In the confusion, he rears up and I'm thrown to the ground...

How to choose a warhorse

A top-class war horse can be very costly to buy and look after, so do pick the right one. It needs to be big, brave and powerful – the finest come from Italy or Spain. Make sure it's barded (well-dressed) in a chanfron (head guard), mail coat and cloth cover displaying your coat of arms. Then choose a suitably war-like name.

At the Battle of Crécy in 1346, the English archers brought down charge after charge of French knights on horseback, and won a crushing victory. Around 4,000 French troops were killed.

Hand-to-hand Combat

I pick myself up and look around. I'm behind enemy lines, in the **mêlée**. The other knights have dismounted too, and we're getting ready to fight on foot with our swords. It's my first taste of hand-to-hand fighting.

It's chaos! The noise is terrible – men yelling and horses squealing. But all those years of sword-fighting practice are paying off. The French are no match for us and we're pushing them back... we just need to stand our ground and pray that we come out of this alive. Wish I knew where Bayard is!

How to survive a mêlée

Fighting in a mêlée is dangerous, however well-prepared you are. These tips could save your life:

1 Stay close to your companions. If you're cut off, you'll be cut down.

2 Don't get caught in the middle – you'll be trampled if there's a push from behind.

3 Stay in one place and fight – moving in your armour will tire you out.

WARNING!

Don't be too much of a hero and get yourself killed. You're worth more alive than dead.

Siege weapons

Never try to attack a castle without the right equipment. This is when you bring out your big guns...

• **Scaling ladders** – set them against the castle walls and climb up. But you run the risk of being pushed off or drenched in boiling water or oil.

• **Siege tower** – wheel it up to the castle walls, then climb up the tower inside, lower the wooden bridge and jump over.

• **Battering ram** – use it to break down walls and doors (the soldiers inside are protected by a wooden roof).

• **Trebuchet** (see left).

Taken Prisoner

Just when things were going so well, disaster struck. We dug some tunnels underneath the castle walls, and the earl sent me to lead a secret **foray**. But I took a wrong turn and was captured, and now they've thrown me into this dungeon. It's cold and damp, and there are rats everywhere. Still, I won't be here for long. They've demanded a ransom of 500 **florins** from the earl to let me go, and he's bound to pay up. Isn't he? I'm lucky, really. If I'd been a common soldier, they'd have just cut my throat.

Getting a ransom paid can be tricky. Wars are costly, and there might not be much cash left in your lord's coffers. There are various places to go for help. Sometimes, the soldiers themselves will club together to raise the money, or the king might meet the cost.

According to the rules of chivalry, captured knights are sometimes kept in a comfortable castle room. For the ransom's sake, it's important to keep them healthy. After all, a prisoner's worth nothing dead.

Capturing a high-ranking prisoner can be like winning the lottery. And if money's hard to come by, you can try demanding the ransom in silver plate, or even wine, instead.

How to demand a ransom

You can make money from your prisoner, but only if you play your cards right.

1 Fix a realistic sum for your ransom, not too low or high.

2 Be prepared to barter. You don't want to get stuck with a prisoner you can't sell back.

3 Be patient (to a point). It can take a while to raise the money.

4 To save yourself work, sell your prisoner (and his ransom) on for a fee.

Victory Banquet

The lord always sits at the centre of the high table because he's the most important person there. Everyone else sits in order of importance: the further from the lord, the less important you are.

What a relief! The earl agreed to pay the ransom and I was released. I knew he wouldn't just leave me to rot. Even better, he sent me a horse to ride home on – my faithful Bayard, of course.

Back home in Corfield Castle, we're having a great banquet to celebrate our victory. There's delicious food, plenty of drink, and brilliant entertainment – the earl's definitely treating us. It might be my last feast here for a while. As a reward for my bravery, the earl's granted me some land of my own.

Medieval menu

A feast can last for hours, with so many different dishes, and the kitchen's kept busy. On the menu today there's roast suckling pig, roast peacock, venison pie and eels in sauce, with sweet custard, jelly, marzipan and eggs in pastry for dessert, all washed down with warm wine.

How to be remembered

You're glad to be back in one piece, but you might not be so lucky next time. In case the worst happens, here's how to make sure people remember your knightly deeds:

1 Give a good donation to the Church for masses to be said when you're dead.

2 Make plans for the grandest tomb you can afford, with a full-size effigy (image of you).

3 Get someone to write a book about you, showing you in the best possible light.

A banquet can get messy. You eat with your fingers, or use a knife and spoon. Instead of a plate, you have a trencher (a slice of stale bread). After the meal, the trenchers are given to the poor.

Ten knotty Knight facts

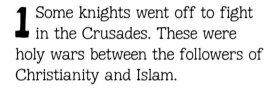

1 Some knights went off to fight in the Crusades. These were holy wars between the followers of Christianity and Islam.

2 Trainee knights gave each other piggybacks to practise fighting on horseback.

3 The wooden swords that knights used in training often weighed more than metal ones, to build up the knights' upper-body strength.

4 A disgraced knight had his spurs taken away and his shield hung upside down.

5 At a tournament, ladies gave 'favours' – scarves, veils or sleeves – to their favourite knights.

6 A jousting lance had a crown-shaped metal cap with three little blunted metal prongs.

7 A servant called a kipper was sent to collect a knight's winnings at a tournament.

8 Most knights owned two or three horses: a warhorse, a palfrey (for riding and hunting) and a packhorse.

9 Some knights trained their warhorses to bite and kick on command – useful in battle.

10 A knight's armour was a status symbol. The better the quality, the more important the knight.

Glossary

Cavalry

Soldiers who fight on horseback

Chivalry

Rules of behaviour that knights had to follow in battle and in life

Florin

A gold coin used in England and Europe

Foray

A sudden attack or raid into enemy territory

Lists

A field near a castle where a tournament was held. 'Entering the lists' meant competing in the tournament

Manor house

A large house owned by a wealthy knight or lord

Mêlée

Disorganized combat fought at close range

Mustering

Gathering troops in preparation for a battle

Oath

A solemn promise

Page

A young boy who serves a lord or knight, in the hope of becoming a knight himself

Pep talk

A talk given by a leader to encourage people to try, or fight, harder

Renaissance

Historical period from the early 14th to the late 16th century

Squire

The second period of knightly training, after a boy has served as a page for seven years

INDEX

The Author
Anita Ganeri is an award-winning author of educational children's books. She has written on a huge variety of subjects, from Vikings to viruses and from Romans to world religions. She was born in India but now lives in England with her family and pets.

The Artist
Mariano Epelbaum was born in Buenos Aires, Argentina. He grew up drawing and looking at small insects under the stones in the garden of his grandmother's house. He has worked as an art director and character designer for many films in Argentina and Spain.